BETTER BY SATURDAY™
IRON PLAY/LONG GAME

Books in the series

BETTER BY SATURDAY DRIVING
BETTER BY SATURDAY IRON PLAY/LONG GAME
BETTER BY SATURDAY PUTTING
BETTER BY SATURDAY SHORT GAME

BETTER BY SATURDAY™

IRON PLAY/LONG GAME

Featuring Tips by
GOLF MAGAZINE®'s
Top 100 Teachers
with Dave Allen

WARNER BOOKS

NEW YORK   BOSTON

Copyright © 2004 by Time4 Media, Inc.
All rights reserved.

Warner Books

Time Warner Book Group
1271 Avenue of the Americas, New York, NY 10020
Visit our Web site at www.twbookmark.com.

Printed in the United States of America
First Printing: May 2004
10   9   8   7   6   5   4   3   2   1

Library of Congress Cataloging-in-Publication Data
Allen, Dave
Better by Saturday—iron play : featuring tips by Golf magazine's top 100
teachers / Dave Allen.
p. cm.
ISBN 0-446-53258-4
1. Swing (Golf) I. Golf magazine (New York, NY : 1991) II. Title.
GV979.S9A44 2004
796.352'3—dc21   2003010756

Book design by HRoberts Design

CONTENTS

Foreword   vii

Acknowledgments   ix

Introduction   I

CHAPTER 1: PRESWING   3

Improve your grip, posture, and alignment to increase odds before you swing

CHAPTER 2: THE SWING   19

Learn how to take the club back properly, start it down correctly, and release it powerfully

CHAPTER 3: FAIRWAY WOODS   35

Hit more greens with these longer, lighter clubs

CHAPTER 4: SHOTMAKING   45

How to draw, fade, hook, slice, and feather it

CHAPTER 5: TROUBLE PLAY   59

What to do when your ball finds a less-than-desirable lie

CHAPTER 6: TROUBLESHOOTING   75
Locating and eliminating the source of your faults

CHAPTER 7: STRATEGY   89
When to attack and when to back down

CHAPTER 8: PRACTICE   101
Fine-tune your swing and tempo with the help of these drills

Foreword: Better by *When?*

When I heard the concept of this new series of books, "Better by Saturday," my reaction was immediate: "Hey, it's already Friday." But having seen the series, I'm convinced that the promise of its premise is fulfilled in these pages, which feature some of the best instruction you'll find in a month of Sundays.

If you're like many golf lovers I know, you dream of playing every day, try to play every week, and settle for a bit less than that. An occasional eighteen is better than nothing, but with so much time between rounds, it's tough to groove a swing. How can your muscles remember the inside-out path they took to the ball when you hit that huge drive your last time out? How can you hope to improve, knowing that PGA Tour pros pummel hundreds and even thousands of practice balls for every one you hit?

Here's how. This book contains the best, simplest tips we could get from the game's finest teaching pros, GOLF MAGAZINE's Top 100 Teachers. They work with thousands of ordinary golfers every week, as well as with top amateurs and Tour pros. They are the best in the business. And thanks to our Top 100

Teachers, each of the four books in the Better by Saturday series—they cover driving; iron play and the long game; the short game; and putting—is full of advice that will help you play better your next time out. You don't have to change your swing. Just pay attention. It's easy, since these tips are clear and often entertaining. Even golfers who play every day will learn plenty.

It's all here: everything from teeing a ball up to hitting one off hardpan or out of a tough lie in a fairway bunker. If there's a situation or shot that always ruins your score, you'll find the cure in these pages. If your troubles take a new form every time out, you'll still find ways to shoot a lower score this weekend. And after that, you can re-read this volume for further improvement, or pick up another of our "Better by Saturday" books.

Imagine how good you might get by next month.

Kevin Cook
Editor, GOLF MAGAZINE

Acknowledgments

Special thanks to Len Zamora and The Mirabel Golf Club in Scottsdale, Arizona, for allowing us the privilege to take these photographs on the spectacular Tom Fazio–designed championship course, located just down the road from Desert Mountain. A big thanks as well to our model for the putting and full swing books, Travis Fulton, an instructor with the PGA Tour Golf Academy at World Golf Village in St. Augustine, Florida. Travis had to strike just about everything but the Heisman pose in our two days of shooting, and for that we're grateful.

Special thanks also go out to GOLF MAGAZINE photographer Fred Vuich, photographer Gary Newkirk, and GOLF MAGAZINE Associate Editor Greg Midland, without whom I'd have been lost in a sea of instruction tips and notebook paper.

Most important, I'd like to thank GOLF MAGAZINE's Top 100 Teachers, an extremely talented group of people, many of whom I've had the great privilege of working with over the last five years. They've taught me so much about the game—probably too much—and for that, I'm extremely grateful—and resentful. Only kidding.—*Dave Allen*

BETTER BY SATURDAY

IRON PLAY/LONG GAME

Introduction

Why? That was the question the editors of GOLF MAGAZINE asked the Top 100 Teachers for a February 2001 cover story. Why do I hit better shots in practice than on the golf course? Why don't my swing keys last? Why do I miss so many greens? Why is golf so hard to learn to play well?

Chances are, you picked up this book because you have the same questions. Why? Why can't I hit two good shots in a row? Why am I suddenly hitting every iron fat? You need answers quickly, so the next time you slice it right in the trees, you can take action and prevent it from happening again. You want a swing you can repeat under pressure, not one that collapses at the first sign of trouble.

For answers to these questions and more, we've asked the world's best teachers again for help. Over the next 100-plus pages, you'll find tips on the setup (how to guarantee the correct ball position every time) and swing (how to use your belt buckle to make a better turn), as well as some keys to hitting better fairway woods (how to use your chin to sweep the ball off the ground). Should you find yourself in the pines, no problem. There are tips to help you hit it under and around the trees. There is also an entire chapter devoted to troubleshooting. This is your fix-it manual, with ways to diagnose then cure your swing ailments before they have a chance to destroy you.

While it's impossible to cover everything in a topic so broad as the "full swing" (we even had to narrow this book down to iron shots and fairway wood shots; for tee shots, see the "driving" book in the "Better by Saturday" series), we've tried to do so here. There's something for everybody, whether you tend to slice the ball, hook it, top it, or shank it. We've also tried to simulate conditions you might see on the course, because no two rounds of golf are ever the same, and there are shots and situations you haven't seen before. You'll find tips on how to hit out of a divot, how to play off hardpan, and how to hit a ball when it's above or below your feet.

Remember: While you can often ride a red-hot putter or a solid driving day to a decent score, it's no way to play consistently good golf. The clubs you hit into almost every green are your irons and fairway woods. If you can be consistent with these clubs, then you're sure to have more opportunities to score, and that's the name of the game.

CHAPTER 1: PRESWING

Slice-Proof Your Grip Preset the left hand and
forearm in a strong position   4

Squeeze Play Use your lifeline to maintain
firm grip pressure   6

Tall and Steady Set up like a skyscraper
for more stability   8

Side Tilt Set your right shoulder lower
than the left   10

Forward Tilt Point your upper body toward
one o'clock   12

Arm Hang Extend your arms so they point
just in front of your toes   14

Ball Position Stand to the handle to take
the guesswork out   16

Slice-Proof Your Grip

Preset the left hand and forearm in a strong position

A great number of swing faults are caused by a faulty grip, usually one that is too weak (hands rotated to the left—toward the target—on the handle). This leads to an open clubface at the top and, in most cases, an out-to-in downswing path. Hello, slice! Here's an exercise to help you develop a stronger grip (hands rotated away from the target).

Before taking your grip, angle the club in front of you so its leading edge and shaft are roughly parallel to your stance line. Wrap your left hand around the grip so it rests diagonally across your fingers, not your palm. This presets the correct forearm and hand position for a strong grip. You should see at least two knuckles and the label of your glove. Then, add the right hand.

—*Dick Harmon*

QUICK TIP

Keep Your Chin Up

To encourage a good shoulder turn, lift your chin at address. Imagine a second ball outside the original ball, and point your nose at it. Getting your chin off your chest straightens your spine, allowing the shoulders to rotate freely around this axis point. —*Paul Trittler*

Squeeze Play

Use your lifeline to maintain firm grip pressure

Many players virtually let go of the club with the right hand at the top of the backswing. Then, sensing their mistake, they re-grip it, throwing the club away from the body, which leads to poor contact.

To prevent this "casting" motion, maintain a firm grip, squeezing the lifeline of your right palm against your left thumb. Here's how to check this: While taking your grip, place a quarter on top of your left thumb [photo 1]. Close your right palm over the left thumb as you normally do, swing to the top, and stop. Without changing your grip, turn your head to look at your hands. If the quarter stayed in place [photo 2], you maintained good, steady, lifeline pressure. If not, keep practicing this "squeeze play." —*Phil Ritson*

QUICK TIP

Aim the Clubface First

To get in the habit of aligning yourself correctly, try picking out a spot a few feet in front of your ball—directly along your target line—and aim your club-face at the spot. Then blend your stance in around that. You should feel very confident aiming to a spot a few feet in front of the ball. —*Craig Harmon*

Tall and Steady

Set up like a skyscraper for more stability

In order for your arms and body to move freely during the swing, you must start from a relaxed, well-balanced posture at address. Your first thought concerning posture should be setting your stance. As a rule, your insteps should be shoulders-width apart; wider if you like, but never narrower. Think of your body as a skyscraper: If the bottom is not at least as wide as the top, it might fall over.

Your stance should be sturdy and your upper body should feel reactive, as though you could catch a medicine ball without losing your balance. **—*Bill Davis***

QUICK TIP

Heel Power

Center your weight over the insides of your heels. This positions your body weight in the center of the feet and improves balance. If your weight is on the balls of your feet, it tends to move too far toward the toes, which makes it harder to maintain your original posture. *—Gary Smith*

Side Tilt

Set your right shoulder lower than the left

The coiling of the body is controlled by the tilt away from the ball, which is set by the natural position of your hands on the club. If you're right-handed, your right hand is farther down on the shaft than your left; thus, your right shoulder is lower than your left, creating a spine tilt of five to 10 degrees away from the target. Set up in this tilt and maintain it through impact, and the body will remain in the ideal hitting position, with the head behind the ball.

To set a five- to 10-degree tilt, hold a club against your chest with your right hand, the shaft parallel to your spine and the clubhead centered between the knees. Bend forward from the hips and then tilt to the right until the clubhead hits the inside of your left knee. This is the amount of side tilt you want at address.

—Mike Bender

Forward Tilt

Point your upper body toward one o'clock

Good posture is grounded in a forward tilt from the hips—not the waist—of about 30 degrees. If you're not sure how much 30 degrees is, picture yourself standing in the middle of a clockface, with your feet at six o'clock. If your upper torso is the top hand, it should point toward one o'clock. Think of this as your swing's Happy Hour: You should maintain it throughout the swing. This posture prevents you from moving up or down during the swing, and helps guide the club on the correct path, which is at 90 degrees to your spine.

Once you establish the correct forward tilt, make sure all your weight-bearing joints are lined up. The top of your spine, insides of your elbows, kneecaps, and balls of your feet should be aligned vertically. Picture yourself standing on a balance beam. To prevent yourself from falling off, you have to balance out these joints. Leaning too far back (on your heels) or too far forward (on your toes) will tip you off the beam. *—Martin Hall*

Arm Hang

Extend your arms so they point just in front of your toes

One great way to check your posture and the alignment of your shoulders and feet at address is to read your arm hang. Looking from down the target line (use a full-length mirror or have a friend observe), your arms should hang on a line extending slightly in front of your toes. Poor posture takes on one of two forms: If the arms are hanging on a line that points in back of the toes, it means you are too upright and need to bend more from the hips; if your arms hang well out in front of the toes, approaching the target line, you are bending over too far.

As for alignment, your shoulders and feet should be parallel to the target line at address. Viewed from behind, the arms should hang evenly, with the right arm nearly obscuring the view of the left. That's proof that the shoulders are aligned correctly. If your shoulders are open—a common slice fault—the right arm will be hanging closer to the target line than the left. **—Todd Sones**

Ball Position

Stand to the handle to take the guesswork out

Many golfers unintentionally change their ball position from shot to shot, which makes it very difficult to put the proper swing on the ball. To guarantee that the ball will be in the correct position for each club, try standing to the handle. In other words, let the club (specifically, its loft) show you where to stand.

First, set the leading edge of the club perpendicular to the target line, with its sole flat on the ground. Then, with your feet close together, stand so the butt end of the grip points just left of your navel [photo 1]. Do not move the handle to fit your body, but move your body into position to fit the handle. Finally, take your stance. As long as the handle points to the same part of your body, ball position is correct. With a driver, the ball will be opposite your front instep; with a 5-iron [photo 2], just ahead of center; with the short irons, near the middle of your stance. **—Donald Crawley**

CHAPTER 2: THE SWING

Proper Takeaway Let the club flow from the start 20

The Right Shift Move the left hip behind the
ball for a fuller shoulder turn 22

Right Over Left Square the face and straighten
your path with this image 24

The "Wait" Shift Let the arms swing down
first before shifting forward 26

Over the Top? Keep your back turned to the
target as the club starts down 28

Perfect Impact Strike a pose to get a feel for a
good impact position 30

Firm Left Side Toe in your left foot to create
a brace for the downswing 32

Proper Takeaway

Let the club flow from the start

Although it's often described in terms of angles and body positions, the golf swing is a single flowing motion. It follows then that the overall shape and tempo of your swing is more important than the individual parts.

To groove a proper takeaway, make some practice swings from a post-impact position [photo 1]. Set up as usual, then extend the clubhead out a few feet past your normal ball position. Start your takeaway from this extended position and continue into your normal swing.

After several practice swings, try hitting balls from this starting position, sweeping the clubhead past the ball and into the takeaway [photo 2]. Starting with good rhythm and a full extension promotes a wide backswing arc, setting the stage for a powerful golf swing. —***Dick Tiddy***

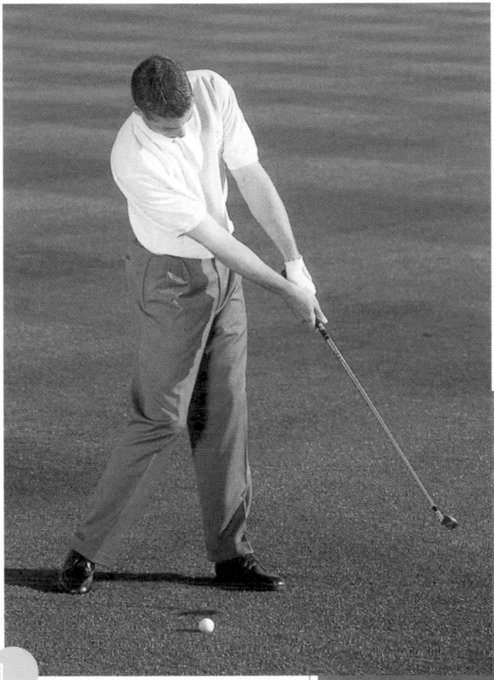

1

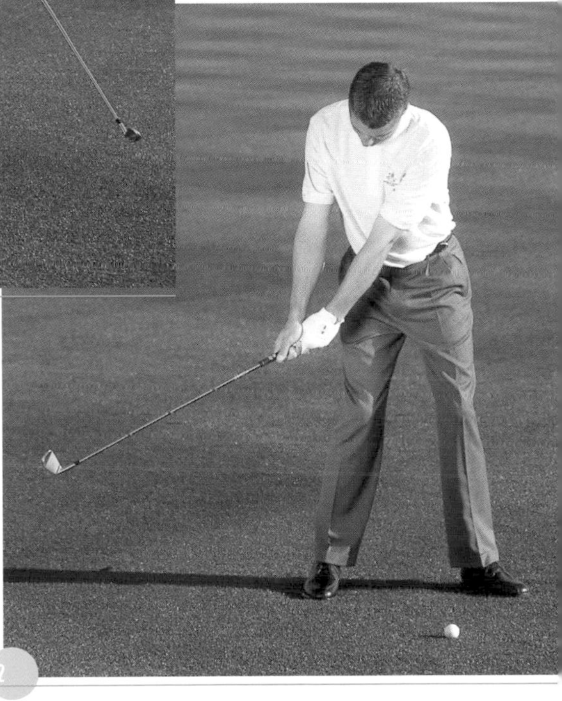

2

The Right Shift

Move the left hip behind the ball for a fuller shoulder turn

In general, golfers are afraid to move laterally off the ball. They think they'll make better contact if they keep their lower body as fixed as possible during the swing. Unfortunately, freezing the lower body usually leads to a reverse weight shift—onto the front foot going back and shifting to the back foot coming through—as well as an abbreviated backswing turn.

To promote the proper lower body action in the backswing, take several practice swings, stopping at the top and feeling as if your belt buckle is over the inside of your right knee. (If you're not very flexible, let the left heel come off the ground.) The key is to move your left hip away from the target a full 45 degrees. This unrestricted hip motion serves two critical functions: First, it deposits your body weight onto the right leg; and second, it promotes a full shoulder turn. With your weight loaded and body coiled, you're ready to make an aggressive move back to the ball.

—*Robert Baker*

Right Over Left

Square the face and straighten your path with this image

Good contact flows from a good backswing. Take the club away on the correct path, and you're in position to return it on the same path—without having to make compensations during the forward swing.

However, many golfers start the club back too far inside—behind the body—fanning the clubface open. This narrows the swing arc and prevents a proper shoulder turn. For a good backswing, keep the right forearm above the left as the arms swing back. Never allow the left arm to get higher than the right. Keeping the right arm on top has three benefits: (1) It allows the arms and body to stay connected, creating maximum extension; (2) it prevents the club from getting stuck behind the body, so it can swing down freely on the correct path; and (3) it places the clubface in a square position at the top of the backswing. —***Mike McGetrick***

The "Wait" Shift

Let the arms swing down first before shifting forward

The last critical moment when the swing can go off-track is in the transition from backswing to downswing. Once the club starts down, the swing is on autopilot and it becomes very difficult to make adjustments.

The proper downswing sequence lets the arms swing down in front of the body, which is critical to squaring the clubface. For this to occur, you need to "wait" momentarily with your torso and lower body as your arms start down, followed by your body shifting toward the target. As the arms drop down, keep your foot pressure directed downward into the ground, as if you were pushing up casual water around your shoes. This forces you to keep your knees flexed and your heels down, limiting the weight shift until the arm swing is well under way. **—*Dr. Jim Suttie***

QUICK TIP

Go to the Backhand

Similar to a left-handed backhand shot in tennis, the left forearm should rotate through the shot and then fold at the completion of the swing. Most of your weight should finish on the outside of your left foot. *—Mitchell Spearman*

Over the Top?

Keep your back turned to the target as the club starts down

For most middle to high handicappers, an over-the-top move—where the right shoulder rushes the clubhead out across the target line before the club has a chance to start downward—results in a slice; for better players, a pull. In all cases, it spells trouble.

One simple concept can quickly cure this nagging swing flaw: Feel as if you keep your back turned to the target at the start of the downswing. When you do, your arms will drop the clubhead inside the target line. Then, when you turn your upper body toward the target, the clubhead is delivered from the inside, and it will be on a shallower path to impact—the right approach for accuracy.

To check this, make your downswing in slow motion. When the club is halfway down, you are in the correct position if a line through your shoulders points to the right of the target. **—*Dick Harmon***

QUICK TIP

Play Shortstop

To trigger the downswing, think about shifting your weight from the back foot to the front, like a shortstop throwing a ball to first base. A natural weight shift will clear your hips properly, so you swing the club through fluidly with a smooth, athletic motion.

—*Rick Whitfield*

Perfect Impact

Strike a pose to get a feel for a good impact position

Impact lasts a fraction of a second, but if you're even slightly out of position, that long, straight shot you visualized will remain merely a vision. That's why you should train for the feeling of perfect impact.

Practice posing your body in the ideal impact position. Growing familiar with it will make you better equipped to repeat it at the moment of truth. First, assume your address position, then move most of your weight onto the outside of your left foot. Keeping your head still, drop your right shoulder slightly and move your hands toward the target. Allow the shaft to tilt forward while keeping the clubface squarely behind the ball. This last point is important because in a good impact position, the shaft is angled much farther toward the target than it is at address. —*Laird Small*

Firm Left Side

Toe in your left foot to create a brace for the downswing

Think of a batter in baseball stepping into a pitch, planting his front foot and firing the bat into the ball. This is precisely the type of braced position you need on the downswing. The front foot should feel as if it is set in cement and the left leg frozen to support the motion of the arms and upper body. This firm left side creates a powerful leverage position, from which your arms can sling the club through the ball, the shaft swinging into a straight line with the left arm at impact.

If you're having trouble feeling a firm left side, turn your left foot slightly inward at address [photo 1]. This toed-in position prevents your left hip from spinning open and your weight from drifting too far toward the target. Practice slow half-swings at first. You'll immediately feel your left side acting as a brace for the downswing, allowing the arms to pass in front of your chest and release the club [photo 2]. —*Mike Malaska*

QUICK TIP

Keep Your Backswing Compact

Swing to the three-quarter point and no farther with your long irons. Making a compact swing prevents you from overhinging the wrists at the top, then casting the hands at the start of the downswing.

—*John Gerring*

QUICK TIP

"Catch the Raindrops"

Here's a great image from the late Paul Bertholy to help you release the club properly: As you swing the clubhead through the hitting area, imagine you're turning the palm of your left hand toward the sky so that, if it were raining, you'd be able to "catch the raindrops."

This exercise encourages a full release—where the right forearm rotates over the left—so the clubface is square at impact and closing shortly after. If this rotation is restricted, the left palm will point at the ground after impact. *—Martin Hall*

CHAPTER 3: FAIRWAY WOODS

Club Design Start with the shaft vertical at address
to maximize loft   36

On the Level Strike a match with the clubhead
for solid contact   38

Stop the Tops Place your hands under your
chin for a wider, sweeping swing   40

Fluffy Lies Hover the club and skim the
top of the grass   42

Club Design

Start with the shaft vertical at address to maximize loft

A fairway wood generates distance with the length of its shaft and the loft of its face. Mis-hits occur when golfers try to create distance with a hard, fast swing. Since the yardage potential is already in the club, swing it with the same effort you would a 7-iron.

The most important aspect of a fairway wood swing is a level path at impact. That starts at address with the shaft nearly vertical and the ball one inch behind your front heel. If you lean the shaft away from the target at address, you're trying to help the ball up in the air. If you lean the shaft toward the target, you're trying to hit down on the ball. Instead, start vertical and let the loft lift the ball and the shaft send it a long way. **—Mark Wood**

On the Level

Strike a match with the clubhead for solid contact

The secret to hitting solid fairway woods and long irons is to swing into impact with a shallow arc that stays low to the ground for as long as possible [photos 1 and 2]. This puts the clubhead's speed directly into the back of the ball for maximum distance and accuracy.

To create this extended flat spot through the hitting area, imagine there is a match attached to the heel and another to the toe of your clubhead [see illustration]. Each is positioned so that the match head sits level with the sole of the club. Also imagine that the ball is resting on sandpaper. As you swing, pretend you are striking both matches as you strike the ball. *—**Martin Hall***

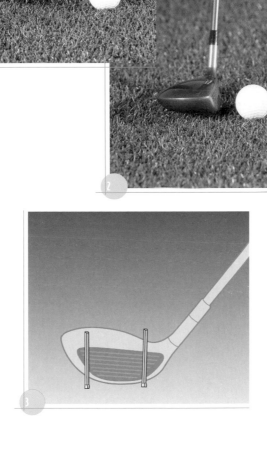

Stop the Tops

Place your hands under your chin for a wider, sweeping swing

Amateurs frequently top or mis-hit fairway woods because of a poor setup: They bend over too much, which positions the hands too close to the body. This inhibits a proper upper-body coil at the top of the backswing. Without a good coil, the downswing becomes too steep.

At address, let your hands hang down from your shoulders so the heels of your hands are in line with your chin. The ball, the club's handle, and your hands should all be positioned just inside the crease on your left pant leg, with the left arm and shaft forming a straight line. This setup allows you to make a wide, elliptical swing for a level-to-slightly-ascending blow at impact. —*Patti McGowan*

QUICK TIP

Take It Wide

Focus on turning the left shoulder level and then around the body on the backswing (not down and under). The arms will follow the turning torso, so that at the top, the club is set to sweep into impact.

—*Bruce Hamilton*

Fluffy Lies

Hover the club and skim the top of the grass

If your ball is sitting up in the rough, beware: This lie can be trouble for a utility wood. These smaller-headed clubs, and the newer shallow-faced woods, can slide right under the ball, especially if you make a steep swing.

When you encounter a "fluffy lie," you can still use these clubs. Simply adjust your setup and swing slightly to create a level approach that allows the clubhead to skim the top of the grass. Position the ball opposite your front heel and divide your weight evenly between your feet. Most important, hover the clubhead slightly above the ground: Do not press it into the grass. Make a wide takeaway with the shaft and left arm staying long as your left shoulder turns. On the downswing, sweep the ball off the top of the rough. **—Donald Crawley**

QUICK TIP

Flare the Left Foot

The longer the club, the more the left foot is turned out. This presets the rotation toward the target on the downswing. The left hip clears faster, which allows the club to return on a flatter plane. **—Scott Sackett**

CHAPTER 4: SHOTMAKING

Fades and Draws Use the hours on a clock to
shape the ball in both directions — 46

Highs and Lows Look up, look down to control
the ball's trajectory — 48

Intentional Curves Hood the face for a hook;
lead with the heel for a slice — 50

Pressure Points Change your grip pressure to
hit different shots — 52

No Speeding When to use your slower clubhead
speed to your advantage — 54

In-Between Clubs Swing shorter back, shorter
through to gear down — 56

Fades and Draws

Use the hours on a clock to shape the ball in both directions

Picture a clock lying on the ground, with the target line running from 6 to 12 o'clock. To hit a fade, a controlled shot that flies left to right, swing the club from 5 to 11. Begin by aiming the clubface where you want the ball to finish (12 o'clock), then aim your body slightly left, where you want the ball to start. Swing along your body line from 5 to 11 [photo 1]. Because the clubface is open relative to the clubhead's path at impact, it will impart left-to-right sidespin on the ball, curving the ball back to 12.

To hit a draw, a controlled shot that flies right to left, simply rotate your body about 10 minutes to the right (clockwise) on the clockface. Aim the clubface at 12 o'clock, then align your body where the ball should start, just right of the target toward 1 o'clock. Swing the club along your body line from 7 to 1 [photo 2]. Because the clubface is closed relative to the path at impact, the ball will start to the right of the target line and curve back to 12.

—*Kevin Walker*

1

2

Highs and Lows

Look up, look down to control the ball's trajectory

You can control the trajectory of your shots simply by adjusting your eyes at address. To hit it high, look up to the sky where you want the ball to reach its maximum height [photo 1], then hold that posture and return your eyes to the ball. Looking high will lower your right shoulder, set most of your weight on your right side, and encourage a shallow swing path. You'll hit the ball with the club's full loft, directing the shot toward the spot you picked out.

To hit it low, look at a low spot along your intended ball flight [photo 2]. This will set your shoulders nearly level and place more weight on your left side, promoting a steeper angle of attack. You'll trap the ball at impact with a delofted clubface, producing a low trajectory. —*Paul Trittler*

QUICK TIP

Take One More to Draw

Use one more club (i.e., a 5-iron vs. a 6) when shaping the ball from right to left. The longer club encourages a freer swing and more clubface rotation through impact—essential to a draw. With less club and a hard swing, the rotation of the club may be restricted, promoting a push or slice. —*Paul Marchand*

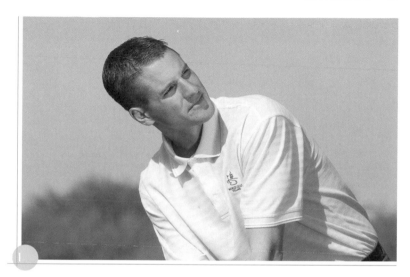

Intentional Curves

Hood the face for a hook; lead with the heel for a slice

Punching out is often your best strategy from the trees, but sometimes you see an opportunity to go for it—if you can curve the ball. Here's how to bend it around a tree or other obstacle on command.

To hit an intentional hook, begin by aiming your feet and shoulders slightly right of the trouble. Next, hood the clubface so it appears to be pointing at your left shoe [photo 1]. Swing normally, making sure to start the downswing with the lower body. This drops the club to the inside, on a hook path.

To hit an intentional slice, begin by aiming your feet and shoulders slightly left of the trouble. Next, open the clubface so the heel is in front of the toe. Finally, swing hard and hang on [photo 2]. You don't want the clubface to turn over, so try and hold off the club's rotation and make the heel lead the toe through impact. **—Rick Whitfield**

Pressure Points

Change your grip pressure to hit different shots

Right-to-left spin, coupled with the lower trajectory of a draw, will add yards to your drives and provide easier access to far-left pin positions. The essential element to hitting a draw is the rotation of the clubface from open to closed through impact. To ensure this occurs, grip the club lightly with your left hand and firmly with your right. This helps the right forearm rotate over the left forearm [photo 1] through impact, closing the clubface.

To fade the ball from left to right on a higher trajectory, good for attacking those far-right pin positions, grip the club firmly with your left hand—applying most of the pressure with the last three fingers [photo 2]—and lightly with your right hand. This will delay the forearms' rotation through impact long enough to keep the face slightly open, curving the ball to the right. For a low shot, grip the club firmly with both hands. Make a smooth swing and keep your grip pressure firm throughout, making sure to lead with your hands through impact. —*Peggy Kirk Bell*

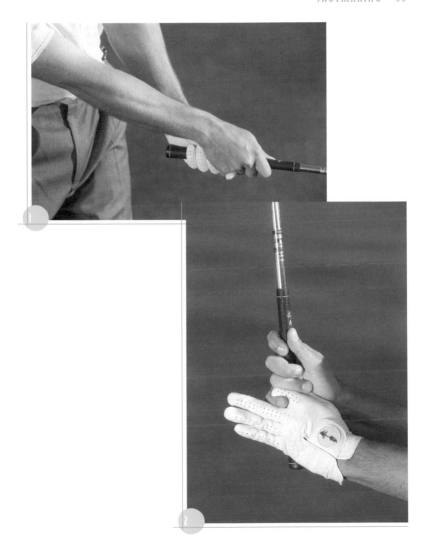

No Speeding

When to use your slower clubhead speed to your advantage

The more clubhead speed you generate, the more backspin the ball has and the higher it flies. Yet, most mid- to high handicappers swing their clubs, on average, about 85 mph, not enough speed to take the high road over a tree or carry the ball on the green from deep rough. On the other hand, there are a number of shots where a slower clubhead speed can be used to a golfer's advantage. Here are just a few:

Driver off deck (uphill lie): Hitting off an upslope increases the driver's effective loft, making it play like a 3-wood. Plan for a shot that flies relatively low and rolls about 25 yards or so—i.e., make sure the green is open in front.

Five-iron from 125 yards (heavy rough): Too much grass between the clubface and ball will prevent you from stopping a 9-iron or pitching wedge on the green, so try to chase a 5-iron up there. The less-lofted club will produce a low shot that flies about 100 yards and rolls onto the green.

Seven-wood from 150 yards (heavy rough): The utility wood's big head will cut through the blades of grass more easily than a mid- or long iron, with enough loft to fly the ball close.

—Bill Davis

In-Between Clubs

Swing shorter back, shorter through to gear down

How many times during the course of a round are you left with a yardage that puts you in-between clubs? Probably more often than you'd like. Do you take the shorter, more-lofted club and apply something extra, or do you take the longer club and "feather" it up there?

In most cases, unless your adrenaline is really pumping or the pin is tucked up front, you should feather it. Take one more club (i.e., a 6-iron instead of a 7-iron), grip down about an inch on the handle, and stand closer to the ball. Then, make your swing thought: shorter back, shorter through. Make equal-length swings (about three-quarters) back and through. The shorter the swing, the slower the swing, and the more likely you are to make solid contact. —***Mike McGetrick***

QUICK TIP

Inch Closer for Fade

Stand one inch closer to the ball than normal to promote a more upright swing and a fade. Stand one inch farther from the ball to promote a flatter swing and a draw. —*Bill Moretti*

CHAPTER 5: TROUBLE PLAY

Fairway Bunkers Dig in and choke down to
make your escape   60

Rough Play Make a steep, "V"–shaped swing
to take less grass   62

Tree Trouble Swing slow and finish low to
avoid the limbs   64

Slippery Slopes Adjust your stance, aim,
and ball position for hilly lies   66

Wind Play Reduce the ball's spin rate to keep it down   68

Flyer Lies Take one less club when hitting from
light rough   70

Divot Holes Keep your hands ahead to ensure
crisp contact   72

Fairway Bunkers

Dig in and choke down to make your escape

From fairway bunkers, most golfers struggle to make good contact. They either take too much sand and hit it short, or else skull it, often into the lip of the bunker. Either way, the result is at least one wasted shot.

Two simple setup adjustments will promote a solid strike. First, twist your feet into the sand until your stance feels stable. Be sure to lower your toes and heels the same depth so your feet are level; this ensures good balance during the swing. Second, choke down on the grip the same amount that you sink your feet into the sand. For example, if you twist your feet down two inches, choke down two inches so the clubface returns to the level of the ball. Now, you're ready to flush it. —*Mark Wood*

QUICK TIP

Don't Drink the Water

When hitting an approach over water, don't let yourself get caught up in the scene. Pick an intermediate target a few feet in front of the ball and make your last look at that spot. Be careful not to look at the water, because every time you do, you get a fresh dose of fear. —*Dr. Richard Coop*

Rough Play

Make a steep, "V"-shaped swing to take less grass

From the rough, you want to make a "V"-shaped swing that will cut the ball out. To do so, position the ball an inch behind the middle of your stance, set 60 percent of your weight over your front foot, and center your head over the ball. Open your stance slightly to encourage a steeper downswing, and open the clubface some to counteract the hosel's tendency to snag in the grass and close the clubface at impact.

Take a few practice swings from a similar lie in the grass to feel the resistance. Then, keep your weight left, cock your wrists early, and make a three-quarter swing. Because perfect contact is unlikely, keep your escape route simple to avoid a big number. **—Scott Sackett**

QUICK TIP

Divide in Half

For a low shot, concentrate on the front (target side) half of the ball. This will set your spine angle slightly toward the target at address and help you keep your hands ahead through impact, minimizing the club's loft and helping create a lower trajectory.

—Laird Small

Tree Trouble

Swing slow and finish low to avoid the limbs

Nobody hits every fairway, so it's important to know how to get out of the trees. Usually the best escape route is under the limbs, with a low shot that reaches the fairway or perhaps even the green. Yet many golfers have trouble deliberately hitting it low, probably because they spend so much time trying to hit the ball into the air.

The secret to the low shot is a slow swing speed, which gives the shot less backspin so the trajectory stays low. Set up with the ball behind the center of your stance and your hands ahead of it, then make a 60 percent swing in length. Focus on rhythm and balance, keeping weight on your left side throughout the swing to limit its length and pace. Finish with your hands low to ensure a low flight. —***Kent Cayce***

QUICK TIP

Handling Hardpan

Playing off hardpan is similar to hitting a 9-iron chip-and-run; you must keep your hands in front of the clubhead through impact. This allows you to catch the ball first, before the ground, utilizing the club's leading edge. —*Mike Bender*

Slippery Slopes

Adjust your stance, aim, and ball position for hilly lies

When the ball is above your feet, the shot will try to hook left. To compensate, stand farther from the ball [photo 1], and set your weight over the balls of your feet. Aim slightly right of the target, and swing at 75 percent of your maximum effort.

When the ball is below your feet, it will try to slice. Grip toward the end of the club, stand closer to the ball [photo 2], and place your weight back on your heels. Take a more-lofted club to reduce the amount of slice and to help get the ball airborne. Aim left of the target, and, once again, swing at 75 percent of your maximum effort.

From an uphill lie, the shot will tend to fly high and short, so use a less-lofted club than normal to lower the trajectory of the shot. Downhill, the shot will tend to fly low and long, so take a more-lofted club than normal to get the ball in the air. In both instances, angle your body to match the slope and position the ball toward the higher foot: front foot on an uphill lie [photo 3]; back foot on a downhill lie [photo 4]. —*John Geertsen Jr.*

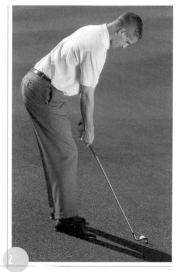

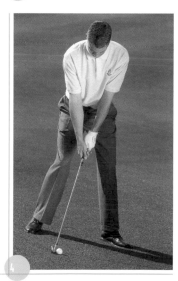

Wind Play

Reduce the ball's spin rate to keep it down

When playing into the wind, try and reduce the ball's spin as much as possible to create a lower, more penetrating ball flight. The higher the ball's spin rate, the higher its trajectory and the more susceptible it is to the wind. To decrease spin, play the ball slightly behind its normal position, with your weight favoring your left side. Take at least one more club, and make a three-quarter-length backswing, swinging at a nice easy tempo.

Match your swing shape to the trajectory you want. Many golfers mistakenly try to create a knockdown shot with a steep swing, hitting down on the ball. This creates even more spin. Envision a ladder standing in front of you, and swing into the rung of the ladder you'd like to hit the ball through. To keep the ball low, envision yourself swinging into a lower rung. *—Kevin Walker*

Flyer Lies

Take one less club when hitting from light rough

Many amateurs approach a shot from light rough [photo 1] (i.e., a flyer lie) as if it were heavy rough. They take the club back very steep, then pull it almost straight down—and hard—stopping the swing at impact. That technique might work from the thick stuff, but when the rough isn't too bad, it leads to a fat shot.

Playing an iron out of light rough should be nearly the same as hitting from the fairway, with one key difference: Take one less club [photo 2] (e.g., a 7-iron versus a 6-iron), because grass will come between the clubface and ball at impact, causing the shot to travel farther with more velocity and less spin. With the right club, set up square, swing on your normal inside-square-inside path (at your normal pace), unwind your hips and shoulders, and be sure to swing through the ball. **—Butch Harmon**

Divot Holes

Keep your hands ahead to ensure crisp contact

Few things in golf are more frustrating than hitting a good drive and then finding your ball sitting down in a divot hole. A key to hitting from a divot—or any other trouble spot—is approaching the situation with a positive attitude. Without good thoughts, chances of success are small.

Take one less club (e.g., a 7-iron for a normal 6-iron shot), play the ball about an inch behind the midway point in your stance, and set about 60 percent of your weight on your left foot. These actions promote a more upright swing. To ensure crisp contact, set your hands ahead of the club [photo 1] and hold that angle throughout the swing. Strive for a full follow-through by swinging your hands up. They should finish level with your left shoulder [photo 2]. —*Shelby Futch*

CHAPTER 6: TROUBLESHOOTING

Hosel Hits Hit the near ball to make the shanks disappear   76

Fat and Thin Shift your weight forward to avoid
these mis-hits   78

Banana Ball Get the toe to beat the heel to defeat a slice   80

Duck Hook Swing the arms to the left to tame a hook   82

Ground Balls Focus on your posture and takeaway
to stop the tops   84

Reverse Pivot Flare out the right foot for a fuller hip turn   86

Hosel Hits

Hit the near ball to make the shanks disappear

A shank occurs when the hosel—that part of the clubhead that connects to the shaft—contacts the ball at impact. Because the hosel is round and has no loft, it sends the ball shooting off-line, usually low and to the right.

The only reason for this ugliest of misses is that the hands are farther from the body at impact than at address. To reel your hands in, try the following drill: Place two balls side by side on the ground, one slightly farther from you. Set up so you're addressing the ball farther away, then swing and hit the closer ball. If you can consistently hit the near ball, you're breaking the habit of moving the arms away from your body during the swing. Remember, any time the shanks appear, the arm swing must be changed. **—*Martin Hall***

QUICK TIP

Size Up Your Grips

If the grips on your clubs are too small, the last three fingers of your left hand will dig into your palm. This causes excess hand action during the swing, which closes the face too rapidly through impact. If the grip is too large, your arms and hands will rotate too slowly, often resulting in a slice. Your grip size is correct if the middle two fingers of your left hand lightly contact your left palm. **—*Kent Cayce***

Fat and Thin

Shift your weight forward to avoid these mis-hits

Laying the sod over the ball (i.e., hitting it fat) can be traced to keeping weight on the back foot for too long during the downswing. Many amateurs struggle with this because they try to help shots into the air and the club bottoms out behind the ball.

When practicing, try to feel the forward weight shift earlier. Address the ball with your feet together, and keep them together as you swing to the top. As the club starts down, step toward the target with the front foot [photo 1] to initiate the forward weight shift. Re-create this feeling during a round by setting up with your left heel off the ground [photo 2]. Make your normal backswing, then, to start the downswing, slam your left heel to the ground.

If your tendency is to hit the ball thin, address the ball with your back heel off the ground [photo 3], and think "chest over right hip over heel" as you swing to the top. (Your heel will drop to the ground as you shift your weight back.) You'll make a better backswing and naturally shift your weight forward on the downswing. —*T. J. Tomasi*

Banana Ball

Get the toe to beat the heel to defeat a slice

The main cause of a slice is an open clubface, often made worse by an out-to-in swing path. Most golfers swing out-to-in because they open their hips and shoulders too quickly at the start of the downswing, which forces the arms to swing across the body.

To correct this problem, focus on rotating the toe of the club inward on the downswing. You should feel as if the toe reaches the ball before the heel does. This aggressive rotation forces you to swing down more with your arms, instead of your hips and shoulders. It also encourages the forearms and hands to rotate the clubhead sooner, which will help to square the clubface at impact. As a result, you'll be hitting more right-to-left draws and fewer slices. **—Dick Tiddy**

QUICK TIP

One Thought at a Time

During a bad stretch, focus on a single positive thought that has worked for you in the past. Try a tempo-inducing cue, such as "low and slow on the takeaway," since most golfers tend to quicken their pace during times of uncertainty. Staying relaxed and recalling past successes are critical when you're trying to find your game again. **—Dr. Richard Coop**

Duck Hook

Swing the arms to the left to tame a hook

For the average golfer, hooks usually follow poor fundamentals: an overly strong grip, hands that begin too far in front of the ball, and an extreme in-to-out swing path. All contribute to and magnify one another.

To tame an out-of-control hook, start by putting your grip in neutral [photo 1]. Check this by taking your address position and cocking your wrists so the club is in front of your body; the face should be square. Then fix your path by focusing on the motion of your arms after impact. Rather than swinging out to the right, think about moving the arms left and across the body into the finish [photo 2]. For the slicer, this is a bad move, but if you're duck-hooking it, swinging the arms to the left encourages more torso rotation through impact, delivering the clubhead down the target line. **—Kip Puterbaugh**

Ground Balls

Focus on your posture and takeaway to stop the tops

There's a misconception among most players, particularly beginners, that a topped shot is caused by "lifting up." That's not exactly true. Most topped shots can be traced to a flaw in the setup or takeaway.

Standing too far away from the ball is one. It forces you to reach for the ball, which produces tension in the arms. When the arms are tense, the muscles contract, which has the effect of shortening them, pulling the club away from the ball. At address, bend forward from the hips until your shoulders are over your toes. Keep the spine as straight as possible. This gives the arms ample room to swing naturally.

Once your setup is solid, check your takeaway. Some golfers lift the club up with their arms, like an axe. You must learn to take the club back low to the ground along the target line. This encourages making a swing with a long flat spot at the bottom of the arc, maximizing your margin for error. To groove a low takeaway, place an extra ball directly on the target line about six inches behind the ball you're hitting. Push the extra ball back as you make your takeaway. **—Bill Moretti**

Reverse Pivot

Flare out the right foot for a fuller hip turn

A good setup "presets" the positions you want to achieve during the swing. We often hear this with regard to grip, posture, and alignment. But don't overlook the right foot; its position at address affects how far the hips can turn on the backswing and ultimately how much power you create.

At address, angle the right foot out 20 degrees—most golfers already do this with the left foot. Turning out both feet slightly opens the knees, which creates a solid support system for the upper body. On the backswing, the right hip easily rotates away from the ball, setting up a full hip turn. This toed-out position also helps keep the hips level and the right leg flexed throughout the swing. If the right foot is perpendicular to the target line at address, the right hip tends to slide laterally and raise up, leading to a reverse pivot (spine tilts toward the target at the top, setting up a steep, arms-only downswing). *—Rina Ritson*

CHAPTER 7: STRATEGY

Par 3s Take one more club when playing to back pins   **90**

Wind Play Stick with your natural shot shape
     when it's blustery   **92**

Lay-Up Plan Avoid partial shots when playing it safe   **94**

Where to Aim Line up to a starting point, not the flag   **96**

Where to Miss Stretch your targets to ensure a safe shot   **98**

Par 3s

Take one more club when playing to back pins

Course architects often use par 3s as "signature holes," challenging players with water hazards, treacherous bunkers, and small targets that offer difficult pin placements. To take advantage of these good scoring opportunities, consider:

- If you're hitting to a two-tier green and the pin is on the bottom level, always take the lesser club. Even if you finish short of the green, you'll face a relatively easy chip. If the pin is back, take more than enough club. That way, if you don't hit the ball solidly, you'll still reach the top shelf. And if you do hit it on the screws, you'll just be over the back where, on most par 3s, there's no trouble.

- If the pin is left and you fade the ball, start your ball at the hole and let it curve into the fat of the green or, at worst, the right fringe, from which you have a good chance of getting up and down for your par. Those of you who draw the ball should attack the hole only when it's cut on the left. When the pin is right, start at the hole and let the ball drift to the fat of the green or the left fringe. ***—Mike McGetrick***

Wind Play

Stick with your natural shot shape when it's blustery

You can afford to be more aggressive when hitting into the wind. Why? Because a headwind will help stop the ball (it will fly higher, then descend more sharply), assisting in your plans for attack. Estimate how much distance the wind will take off the shot, and use more club. The rule of thumb is to take one extra club for every 10 mph of wind.

When playing into a crosswind, do not deviate from your natural shot shape. If, like most amateurs, your shots curve from left to right, don't try to hit a draw because the wind is blowing from the left. Tee the ball up on the far right side of the tee box and aim down the left side of the fairway, allowing the wind and your shot pattern to turn the ball back into the fairway. Never aim directly at trouble (water, out of bounds, etc.), and always keep the ball low. —***Kevin Walker***

Lay-Up Plan

Avoid partial shots when playing it safe

When was the last time you played a round without laying up?
Probably never. Planning and executing a good lay-up is as
important as any other shot in your bag. Don't take it for
granted.

　　As a rule, don't hit a lay-up that results in a partial swing for
your next shot; you'll always be most confident making a full
swing. However, if the pin is way back, consider laying up closer,
to 30 or 40 yards, so you can use the length of the green to play
a bump-and-run shot to the hole. If the pin is up, always leave a
full wedge, as you'll need the higher trajectory to drop the ball
close. **—Bill Davis**

QUICK TIP

How to Pick a Club

Choosing the right club for an approach shot
requires reading the situation, not just the yardage.
Always figure in: (1) what the distance will actually
play; (2) where you want the ball to end up; and (3)
how well you are swinging. Be realistic about the
last. Don't just grab the club that would get you to
the target on your best shot. *—Mitchell Spearman*

Where to Aim

Line up to a starting point, not the flag

The target—the flag, usually—is such an obvious aiming point that it's where your attention naturally goes. But keep in mind that the target is where you want the shot to end up. Unless you hit the ball dead straight, you don't want to aim there. Instead, aim for where you want the ball to start.

Identify your ball-flight pattern for the shot you're playing, whether it's left to right or right to left, and allow for the curvature with your aim. If you fade the ball, aim at a spot left of the flag, such as a bunker. That's your starting point. If you make your normal swing, the ball will drift right, toward the flag. If you were to aim at the flag and make your normal swing, you would miss the green to the right. Lining up to a starting point, rather than the flagstick, will improve your likelihood of finishing close to the hole. —*Rick Martino*

Where to Miss

Stretch your targets to ensure a safe shot

Do you automatically assume your target is the center of the fairway? Do you always aim for the flag on your approach shots? I've talked to several club pros who have taken all 18 flagsticks out, just for fun, and seen their members shoot lower scores.

Point is, shifting your focus from your target to your "target area" can help. Many holes with hazards on one side are wide open on the other. In these cases, cheat to the trouble-free side to ensure a safe shot. On approaches, see where the trouble lies and borrow a little the other way. In this photo, the target area extends short and left of the hole. Being a good shotmaker is knowing not only where to hit the shot, but also where to miss it. —*Jim Flick*

QUICK TIP

Stick with the Plan

Always have a game plan for how you want to play each hole. What will you hit off the tee? Which side is best to come in from? And, if you do make a big number, don't change your plan. Get back in your comfort zone by going through the same preshot routine, in the same amount of time. Its familiarity will help you regroup. —*Dr. Richard Coop*

CHAPTER 8: PRACTICE

The Inside Track Keep the butt end pointing
right of the target line   102

Speed Drills How to slow down and speed up
your swing's tempo   104

Hilly Solutions Head to the slopes to cure a faulty path   106

Ground Assault Leave a divot that starts ahead of the ball   108

The Inside Track

Keep the butt end pointing right of the target line

No matter what your path problem is, this drill will help you get back on track. Remember, to hit the ball straight, the clubhead must approach the ball from slightly inside the target line, cover the line at impact, and then sweep inside again.

Place a club on the ground just outside your ball and parallel to your target line. Take your normal swing but stop when the shaft is parallel to the ground on the downswing. At this point, the butt end of the shaft should point slightly right of your target, at about a 10-degree angle to the club on the ground. This means the club is approaching from slightly inside the target line, setting up the proper path through impact. As a swing thought, try to drop your right elbow into your right front pocket coming down; this keeps the club to the inside. **—*Dr. Gary Wiren***

QUICK TIP

Tee the Ball

If you're struggling to get the ball airborne on the practice range, tee it up. Seeing the ball fly high breeds confidence. It also allows you to focus more on what your body is doing—"Am I making a good shoulder turn?" "Am I shifting my weight properly?"—and less on getting the clubhead on the ball. **—*Darrell Kestner***

Speed Drills

How to slow down and speed up your swing's tempo

To slow down an overly fast swing, spill out a large bucket of balls on the driving range. Using a 7-iron, make a full swing, trying to hit the first dozen balls about half your normal 7-iron distance (75 yards if your usual 7-iron distance is 150). Next, hit about two-thirds your normal distance (100 yards), then hit a dozen 125 yards. Finally, hit the rest of them the full 150 yards. This drill gives you a feel for swinging at a slightly slower speed with all your clubs. It also allows you to stay in balance and contact the sweetspot of the clubface more consistently.

If you feel the need to speed up your tempo, take out a 7-iron again, and try and hit it your normal distance, making a three-quarter-length swing. Shortening the backswing feels as if you're losing power, so you must speed up your tempo to succeed. After hitting a small bucket of balls with the three-quarter 7-iron, try it with some longer clubs, up to your driver. **—Mike McGetrick**

Hilly Solutions

Head to the slopes to cure a faulty path

Practice from angled lies to help get your swing back on track. If your swing plane is too flat (usually resulting in a hook, push, or topped shot), practice with the ball below your feet. When the ball is below your feet, your spine angle becomes more tilted to address the ball, forcing your shoulders to turn on a more vertical plane during the backswing. During the swing, concentrate on keeping the arms in front of your body. This should help you deliver the clubhead on a straighter path, and result in more solid contact.

If your swing plane is too upright (usually resulting in a slice, pull, or topped shot), practice hitting balls well above your feet. When the ball is above your feet, your spine angle will become more vertical, forcing your shoulders to swing on a flatter plane. The key is to allow your arms to rotate during the swing—in the follow-through, the right forearm will rotate over the left. Done correctly, you'll make solid contact with the back of the ball from inside the target line and the result will be a longer-flying, right-to-left draw. **—Peter Krause**

Ground Assault

Leave a divot that starts ahead of the ball

Except for ball flight, your divots are the only tangible evidence of how you've swung. If your divot starts behind the ball, the club has bottomed out too soon, usually the result of an overly steep swing on an outside-in path.

Practice taking divots that start ahead of the ball. Stick a tee several inches outside but even with the back of the ball [photo 1]. Take your 7-iron and try to swing it on an approach that is inside the target line on a shallow, slightly descending path. If you're properly transferring your weight forward and hitting the center of the clubface, the club will bottom out ahead of the ball, leaving a divot that starts ahead of the tee [photo 2]. —*Dr. **Gary Wiren***

QUICK TIP

Analyze Your Iron Game

Hit a few dozen shots with a variety of clubs on the practice range, noting your contact with the ball and the flight pattern of your shots. If you hit most of the shots fat, move the ball back in your stance. If you hit most shots thin, move the ball forward. If you're hitting a fade or draw, don't try to correct it—play for it. There's no time for swing tinkering. —*John Gerring*

For more golf tips, as well as news, travel advice, equipment updates, and more, visit **GOLF MAGAZINE** on the web at www.golfonline.com.